Artists in Their Time

Henri Matisse

Jude Welton

Franklin Watts
A Division of Scholastic Inc.
New York Toronto London Auckland Sydney
Mexico City New Delhi Hong Kong
Danbury, Connecticut

First published in 2002 by
Franklin Watts
96 Leonard Street
London EC2A 4XD

First American edition published
in 2002 by Franklin Watts
A Division of Scholastic Inc.
90 Sherman Turnpike
Danbury, CT 06816

Series Editor: Adrian Cole
Series Designer: Mo Choy
Art Director: Jonathan Hair
Picture Researcher: Diana Morris

A CIP catalog record for this title
is available from the Library of Congress.

ISBN 0-531-12228-X (Lib. Bdg.)
ISBN 0-531-16621-X (Pbk.)

Printed in China

Acknowledgments

AKG London:fr cover br, 8, 20tl, 38t. Albright Knox Gallery, Buffalo, NY: Bridgeman 35 ©
Succession H Matisse/DACS 2002. Baltimore Museum of Art, Maryland: Mrs Ethel and Mr
Robert Berney Papers 32b, Bridgeman 33 © Succession H Matisse/DACS 2002. The Barnes
Foundation, Merion: Bridgeman 17 © Succession H Matisse/DACS 2002, Corbis 31t ©
Succession H Matisse/DACS 2002. Bettmann/Corbis: 12b, 14t. Christies Images/Corbis: 41t ©
Romare Bearden Foundation/VAGA, New York/DACS, London 2002. Geoffrey Clements/ Corbis:
40 © Kenneth Noland/VAGA, New York/DACS, London 2002. Alvin Langdon Coburn/Hulton
Archive: 12tl. Corbis: 38bl. Gérard Degeorge/Corbis: 25t. Mary Evans PL: fr cover bl, 9b, 10t, 14b.
Galerie Irus et Vincent Hansma, Paris: 32c. Chris Hellier/Corbis: 34br. Hermitage, St Petersburg:
Artothek 9t, Scala 19 © Succession H Matisse/DACS 2002, Giraudon/Bridgeman 21 ©
Succession H Matisse/DACS 2002. Dave G. Houser/Corbis: 10c. Hulton Archive: 34t. Bob
Krist/Corbis: 20. Gail Mooney/Corbis: 41b. Musée Condé, Chantilly: Giraudon/Bridgeman 24t.
Musée Matisse, Le Cateau-Cambrésis: 6b. Courtesy Lee Miller Archives: 26b. Musée d'Orsay,
Paris: Lauros-Giraudon/Bridgeman 15 © ADAGP, Paris and DACS, London 2002, Roger-
Viollet/Bridgeman 11 © Succession H Matisse/DACS 2002. Museum of Modern Art, New York:
Scala 22 © Succession H Matisse/DACS 2002, 27 © Succession H Matisse/DACS 2002. Musée
National d'Art Moderne, Paris: CNAC/MNAM Dist. RMN 29 © Succession H Matisse/DACS
2002. Photo Archives Matisse: D.R: 6tr, 16c, 18, 20c, 28c, 31b. Private Collection: Bridgeman 7
© Succession H Matisse/DACS 2002, 16tl © Succession H Matisse/DACS 2002. Pushkin
Museum, Moscow: Scala 23 © Succession H Matisse/DACS 2002. Ross Ressmeyer/Corbis: 28tl.
Roger-Viollet/Bridgeman: 42. Stadishes Kunstmuseum, Bonn: Artothek 25b. Statens Museum for
Kunst, Copenhagen: 13 © Succession H Matisse/DACS 2002. Niklaus Stauss/AKG London: fr
cover bc, 37. Tate Picture Library, London: fr cover c & 39 © Succession H Matisse/DACS 2002.
Three Lions/Hulton Archive: 26c. Victoria & Albert Museum, London: Bridgeman 36b.

Whilst every attempt has been made to clear copyright
should there be any inadvertent omission please apply
in the first instance to the publisher regarding rectification.

Contents

Who Was Henri Matisse?

Matisse was one of the greatest and most original artists of the last century, a master of color and flowing line, whose delightful paintings continue to influence the art world today.

Matisse played a leading role in the "modern art" revolution that occurred in the early 20th century, and was famous for his paintings, sculpture, prints, drawings, book illustrations, and costume and stage designs.

▶ A photograph of Henri Matisse and his mother Anna in 1889. "Everything I have done comes from my parents, unassuming, hardworking people," wrote Matisse.

▲ A modern view of Le Cateau-Cambrésis, Matisse's birthplace. This square, the Place du General de Gaulle, is named after the French leader Charles de Gaulle.

There was no hint in Matisse's early life that he was going to have such a dramatic impact on the world of art. Matisse was born on New Year's Eve in 1869, in his grandparents' house in Le Cateau-Cambrésis, a small town in northern France. Henri-Emile-Benoît Matisse was brought up in nearby Bohain. His parents were middle-class shopkeepers, who had a family store that sold grain and paint.

A LAW STUDENT

Little is known about Matisse's childhood and adolescence. He went to the local primary school, and then to the lycée, or secondary school, in the nearby town of Saint-Quentin. It was here that Matisse won first prize in a drawing competition.

In 1887, at age eighteen, Matisse was sent by his parents to study law in Paris. He passed his exams the first time, and returned home two years later to work as a clerk in a lawyer's office in Saint-Quentin.

TIMELINE ▶

1869	1887	1890
Matisse is born at his grandparents' house in Le Cateau-Cambrésis.	Matisse is 18. He moves to Paris to study law.	Matisse is taken ill with appendicitis. While he is recovering he creates his first painting *Still Life With Books* (see page 7).

A TURNING POINT

During the 1890s, typewriters were rare and computers had not been invented, so Matisse's office duties consisted mainly of copying documents by hand, which he found extremely boring.

▲ *Still Life With Books,* 1890
Dark, shadowy, detailed, and realistic, this early painting by Matisse was made when he was twenty-one.

The turning point in Matisse's life and career came in a surprising way – he suffered an acute attack of appendicitis. During the year it took him to recover, he used the paintbox his mother had given him to copy landscapes from a painting manual. By June of 1890, he had made his first painting, *Still Life With Books* (a version of this is shown on the left). When Matisse returned to work after his illness, he also started attending a 7AM-8AM drawing class at the local school for textile designers. He had discovered his vocation. It was not to be a lawyer, but an artist.

"When I started to paint, I felt transported into a kind of paradise."

Henri Matisse

NORTHERN FRANCE

Matisse was born in a town called Le Cateau-Cambrésis, situated north of Paris and just 30 miles (50 km) from the Belgian border. The surrounding area has magnificent Gothic cathedrals, including France's largest at Amiens. The area was famous for agriculture and industry rather than art. However, at museums in Lille, Arras, and Cambrai, Matisse was able to see the paintings of masters such as Goya and Rembrandt. When Matisse was in his forties, it became the scene of devastating trench warfare in World War I (1914-18), which earned it the unfortunate label of "The Battlefield of Europe."

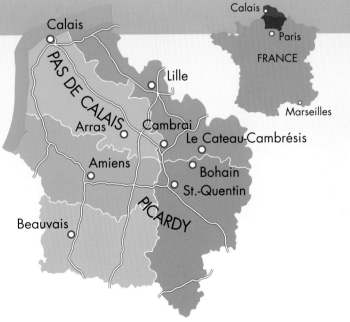

A Student in Paris

In 1891, Matisse's father reluctantly agreed to allow his 21 year-old son to give up his law career and move to Paris to study art. Living on a small monthly allowance from his father, Matisse joined a teaching studio, or academy. Head of staff at the Académie Julian was the then-famous Adolphe Bouguereau. Matisse did not agree with Bouguereau's traditional ideas about art, nor did he enjoy his strict teaching methods. This is why he did not stay there long. Although he was refused admission to the Ecole des Beaux-Arts (Paris's official art school) at first, Matisse was invited to become an "informal" student of the painter Gustave Moreau, who had a teaching studio there. A gentle, enthusiastic teacher, Moreau encouraged his students to express themselves through their art. He also taught them to improve their technique by copying paintings by Old Masters. Matisse was able to earn money by selling the copies he made.

▲ When Matisse arrived in Paris in 1891, it was the cultural capital of Europe. The Paris skyline was dominated by the Eiffel Tower (above), which had been built just a few years earlier, in 1889.

EARLY INFLUENCES

Matisse's early paintings were mostly of quiet interior scenes and landscapes, but in the late 1890s, he rejected traditional painting techniques. His pictures began to change, becoming bolder and more colorful. Paintings he made during trips to Brittany and Corsica show the influence of contemporary artists such as the Impressionists. Matisse could see their bright, loosely painted pictures on display at the new commercial galleries in Paris.

THREE BATHERS

At one of these galleries Matisse bought a painting by Paul Cézanne, *Three Bathers*. Cézanne (1839-1906) did not try to make his pictures look like the real world. He developed a way of using color to build up a sense

TIMELINE ▶

1891	1894	1898	April 1900
Matisse arrives in Paris to study art and joins the Académie Julian.	Matisse's girlfriend, Caroline Joblaud, gives birth to their baby daughter, Marguerite.	Matisse marries Amélie Paraye. In two years they have two sons.	Matisse works as a decorator for the Universal Exhibition which is held in Paris. It attracts over 50 million visitors.

Still Life, Paul Cézanne, c.1895
Cézanne is known as the "father of modern art," because he created a new way of painting. He broke away from the long tradition of artists creating an illusion of the real world. In this picture Cézanne does not try to make the objects on the table look as they do in real life. He is concerned with finding a way to show them together on the painting's flat surface.

"You will simplify painting."

Gustave Moreau to Henri Matisse

of volume and space. Cézanne's paintings had an enormous influence on 20th-century art and on Matisse's art in particular.

NEW RESPONSIBILITIES

During this time, while Matisse was developing his own style and struggling to make a name for himself, he was very poor. His father had stopped his allowance, and he now had a family to support – his girlfriend, Caroline Joblaud, had given birth to a daughter, Marguerite, in 1894. Matisse soon separated from Caroline, and in 1898 he married Amélie Paraye. By 1900, they had two sons, Pierre and Jean.

To support his young family Matisse took a temporary job as a decorator for the Universal Exhibition (see below). He even applied for a job as a tax assessor but he was turned down. Eventually, he took his family home to his parents. However, these difficult times were coming to an end.

THE UNIVERSAL EXHIBITION

The Universal Exhibition was the biggest international exhibition the world had ever seen. It was held in Paris from April to November 1900 and attracted over fifty million visitors. Elaborate pavilions were built across the capital, displaying artistic, scientific, and technological achievements from around the world.

The electrically powered moving staircase, or escalator, recently invented in the U.S., was seen here for the first time. Other modern inventions on display included x-ray photography, wireless telegraphy, and the car. Matisse was part of a huge workforce of architects, designers, sculptors, and painters building and decorating the pavilions.

▲ The spectacular Palace of Electricity formed the centerpiece of the 1900 Universal Exhibition. It was lit by electric light, a recent invention that was beginning to change the look of Paris, as electric street lighting replaced old-fashioned gas lamps.

Early Experiments With Color

▲ Preparations for the opening of the official Salon in Paris, 1902, the year before the Salon d'Automne was founded.

In 1904, Matisse spent the summer in southern France, where he was influenced by the Neo-Impressionist artist Paul Signac (1836-1935). Signac believed that pictures looked brighter when they were painted in dots of pure color. These dots mixed in the viewer's eye rather than on the palette or canvas. Matisse's major Neo-Impressionist work is the harmonious *Luxe, Calme et Volupté* (right). It was exhibited at the Salon des Indépendants in 1905, and bought by Signac, who was delighted to have "converted" Matisse. However, Matisse soon found Neo-Impressionism limiting, and in 1905 his art underwent a complete change.

OFFICIAL AND UNOFFICIAL ART

From the 17th century onward, the official art exhibition in Paris, the Salon, dominated French art. The Salon jury only chose to exhibit "conservative" paintings such as historical, biblical, or mythological subjects. These were painted to look as real as possible. Artists who did not paint in this traditional way were rejected and had nowhere to show or sell their work.

The system became more open in the late 19th century, when the Salon des Refusés was set up by the Emperor Napoleon III in 1863.

Eventually modern artists put on their own exhibitions such as the Salon d'Automne, where the Fauves caused a scandal in 1905.

▲ The picturesque fishing village of Collioure is situated on the French Mediterranean coast, close to the Spanish border. Its maze of narrow streets, restaurants, and secluded beaches have inspired many artists.

BREAKING THE RULES

In 1905, Matisse traveled south again, to the village of Collioure, where he was joined by the artist André Derain (1880-1954). The two men painted excitedly, deliberately disobeying the "rules" of painting, and using color in an imaginative, personal way.

TIMELINE ▶

1901	1903	1904	1905
Matisse begins to exhibit at the Salon des Indépendants.	The Salon d'Automne is established.	Matisse exhibits at Vollard's Gallery. Spends summer in the south of France, where he is influenced by the Neo-Impressionist artist Paul Signac.	Matisse paints with Derain at Collioure. Exhibits with Derain, Albert Marquet, Georges Rouault, Maurice de Vlaminck, and others at the Salon d'Automne. Critics label them the "Fauves."

Luxe, Calme et Volupté, 1904-05

oil on canvas, 37 x 46 in (98.5 x 118 cm), Musée d'Orsay, Paris, France

According to Matisse, the uniform dots and dashes of the "pure rainbow colors"
in this and "all the paintings of that school [Neo-Impressionism] produced
the same effect." He soon moved on to develop his own, freer style.

"We painted like children in the face of nature."

Henri Matisse, on the summer he spent with André Derain at Collioure, 1905

Scandal and Success

In the autumn of 1905, a number of artists, including Matisse and Derain, exhibited their paintings at the Salon d'Automne in Paris. Many visitors were shocked by this new type of art, and the group became known as the "Fauves," which means "wild beasts" in French.

WEALTHY PATRONS

The greatest outrage at the exhibition was caused by Matisse's painting *Woman With a Hat*, 1905 (see page 14). The painting was bought by Leo and Gertrude Stein, wealthy Americans living in Paris. Along with their brother and sister-in-law, Michael and Sarah Stein, they became Matisse's most important early patrons, and introduced him to other collectors and artists including Pablo Picasso.

▲ A photograph of Amélie, taken at Matisse's studio. Compare her hairstyle and neckline with the painting opposite.

AMÉLIE MATISSE

Born Amélie Paraye, in Toulouse, southern France, Madame Matisse was described by her husband as "erect, dignified of bearing, and possessed of splendid dark hair." They married in Paris in 1898, and spent their honeymoon in London.

"Exceptionally devoted, working to enable him [Matisse] to concern himself only with his painting," Amélie took on the role of mother for Matisse's daughter Marguerite, and soon had two sons, Jean and Pierre.

By the mid-1920s Matisse had stopped painting her. He began to spend more time working away from home, visiting his wife only occasionally. The marriage eventually ended in the 1930s.

◄ Gertrude Stein in her Paris apartment, with paintings by Georges Braque and Pablo Picasso. Matisse met Picasso at her apartment, and also Sergei Shchukin, who became another great collector of his work (see page 18).

The Steins bought the daring and unusual portrait opposite, *Madame Matisse*. They renamed it *The Green Stripe*, because of the vivid line of paint that runs down the forehead and nose, almost dividing the face in half. Although it is a recognizable portrait of Amélie, Matisse was less concerned with likeness than with the relationship between areas of color on the canvas.

Madame Matisse (The Green Stripe), 1905

oil on canvas, 15 $^7/_8$ x 12 $^7/_8$ in (40.5 x 32.5 cm), Statens Museum for Kunst, Copenhagen, Denmark

Rather than giving the portrait a realistic "background," Matisse set Amélie's face in a patchwork of violet, orange, and turquoise-green. Along with the dark blue hair, and pink and yellow flesh, these areas make up a powerful but balanced pattern of contrasting colors.

The "Wild Beasts"

The period between 1900 and the outbreak of World War I in 1914, was a time of great excitement and experimentation in the world of art. Just as everyday life was changing, with new inventions such as the car, electric light bulb, and escalator, so many artists were looking for new ways to reflect the modern world in which they lived – going beyond creating paintings that looked like real life.

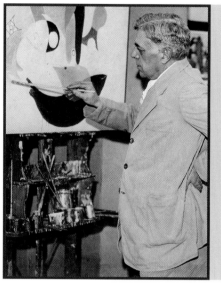

◄ The French artist Georges Braque (1882-1963) was also influenced by the Fauves and for a time (1905-1907) was linked with them. Braque, along with Pablo Picasso, was responsible for creating a new type of art known as Cubism.

▲ This page from the magazine *L'Illustration*, dated November 1905, shows some of the Fauve paintings on show at Le Salon d'Automne that year. Matisse's *Woman With a Hat*, 1905, can be seen center left.

NEW WAYS OF PAINTING

In the past, artists had always tried to create paintings and sculptures that looked like real people, places, and objects. However, the increasing use of photography, developed in the mid-19th century by Louis Daguerre (1789-1851), made many artists eager to experiment with different, less representational styles of painting.

Through Neo-Impressionism, Matisse understood how color in painting did not have to be used in a descriptive, "naturalistic" way. For example, a tree, like that in *Luxe, Calme et Volupté*, 1904-05 (see page 11) might look brown in real life, but in a painting of that tree, the artist could choose to use yellow, purple, pink, red, green, or blue – or all six!

A CIRCLE OF FRIENDS

Working with André Derain in southern France in the summer of 1905, Matisse explored more creative and exciting uses of color. Meanwhile, other friends of Matisse, including Albert Marquet (1875-1947) and Maurice de Vlaminck (1876-1958), were developing their style along similar lines, using bold, contrasting colors and rapid, sketchy brush strokes.

▲ *Charing Cross Bridge*, André Derain, 1905-06
Derain used intensely brilliant, "unnatural" colors and unusual viewpoints. He chose and arranged his colors to make the picture look the way he wanted.

In the autumn, the friends exhibited together at the Salon d'Automne. Their unconventional landscapes and figure paintings caused a public scandal because no one had seen anything like them before, and people were shocked. One critic compared them to "fauves," or wild beasts.

Even though this name was not used by the painters themselves, it created an identity and publicity for the group, which helped sell their paintings. This was the first time that a scandal caused by modern art led directly to commercial success. It also marked a turning point in Matisse's life.

THE FAUVES BREAK UP

The Fauves never considered themselves a formal group. Within a couple of years the individual artists developed their own, differing styles. Although it was short-lived, Fauvism had a broad effect on the development of modern art. It showed how color could be used in a new way, for example, to express feelings. As Matisse wrote, "Fauvism is not everything, but it is the foundation of everything."

The "wild beasts" sowed the seeds of Expressionism and Abstract Art, two of the great art movements of the 20th century.

A Revolution in Color

While the Fauve scandal was still raging, Matisse began work on the largest painting he had ever made. Set in an imaginary, ideal world, *The Joy of Life* (right) shows graceful figures lounging, dancing, and playing music in an unspoiled paradise. The flat areas of yellow, pink, orange, red, green, and blue are not the colors of a real landscape, but are chosen for their decorative effect. Although criticized, even by some of Matisse's friends, the painting came to be seen as a landmark in modern art.

▲ *Reclining Nude II*, 1927 (bronze). Matisse painted and sculpted reclining nudes throughout his life (see pages 11, 17, and 33).

MATISSE'S SCULPTURE

Taking some of the figures from *The Joy of Life* (opposite) as his starting point, Matisse spent much of the winter of 1906-07 making clay sculptures.

Matisse had been sculpting figures and faces for a number of years. For him making sculptures was a way to relax, as well as providing a means of exploring his ideas about form and volume.

Figures, such as *Reclining Nude II*, 1927 (above), were a favorite subject. Sometimes his sculptures appear in his paintings (see page 22).

▲ Matisse (seated, center) was nicknamed "The Doctor" by his students because of his unexpected formality.

MATISSE THE TEACHER

The Stein family continued to support Matisse and even gave him money to start his own art school in Paris. Students at the art school, expecting a wild, revolutionary teacher, were surprised to find that Matisse wanted them to copy ancient Greek statues and study the work of the Old Masters. He stressed that artists needed to learn the rules of color and composition before they could break them. Later, in 1911, feeling he "had to choose between being a painter and a teacher," he closed the school.

TIMELINE ▶

1906	1907	1908
The Joy of Life is exhibited at the Salon des Indépendants; Leo Stein buys it. Matisse visits Biskra in Algeria, meets Picasso at the Steins' apartment. Paul Cézanne dies.	Matisse exchanges paintings with Picasso. Visits Padua, Florence, Arezzo, and Siena in Italy.	Matisse opens his art school in Paris.

The Joy of Life, 1905-06

oil on canvas, 69 $^1/_8$ x 94 $^7/_8$ in (174 x 238 cm), The Barnes Foundation, Merion, Pennsylvania

Look at the way Matisse brings the landscape and figures together, making the gentle curve of the trees echo the lines of the bodies. The ring of dancing figures is a motif that is used several times in Matisse's work (see page 21).

"He clashed his colors together like cymbals and the effect was like a lullaby."

The art critic John Berger writing about Matisse

In Search of Harmony

Matisse's reputation soon spread beyond Paris, and he exhibited paintings in Britain, Germany, Russia, and the United States. His art was especially popular in Russia, possibly because the strong traditions of Russian folk-art meant that people there were used to looking at pictures that were not simply naturalistic portrayals of reality.

SERGEI SHCHUKIN

One of Matisse's most supportive patrons was the Russian merchant Sergei Shchukin, who had met Matisse through the Steins. In 1908, Shchukin bought *Harmony in Red* – although when he bought it, the painting was actually called *Harmony in Blue*. Feeling that the blue color did not contrast enough with the scene through the window, Matisse asked Shchukin to return the painting, and painted over it in red.

A PAINTER'S NOTES

Some artists like to write about their ideas on art, and Matisse wrote a great deal. One of his most famous essays, called "A Painter's Notes," was published in 1908.

In it Matisse wrote, "What I am after, above all, is expression," explaining that he did not mean he wanted to paint faces or gestures showing particular emotions. Instead he wanted his paintings to express what he called "the feeling I have for life" through the way objects, colors, and lines were arranged on the canvas.

Matisse summed up the feeling he wanted his paintings to express, "What I dream of is an art of balance, of purity, and serenity, devoid of any awkward or disturbing subject matter...like a comforting influence, a good armchair in which one rests."

> *"I try to put serenity into my pictures."*
>
> Henri Matisse

▲ One of the rooms in Shchukin's Moscow mansion where his magnificent art collection was housed. Shchukin eventually owned thirty-seven Matisse paintings and a number of works by other artists, including Claude Monet, Paul Gauguin, and Paul Cézanne. Following the Russian Revolution of 1917, the collection was confiscated, and the paintings are now divided between Russia's Pushkin and Hermitage museums.

TIMELINE ▶

1908	1908	December 25, 1908
Matisse travels to Germany, and exhibits in New York and Moscow.	Sergei Shchukin buys *Harmony in Blue* which Matisse then changes to *Harmony in Red*.	Matisse publishes "A Painter's Notes" in *La Grande Revue*. In it he includes practical and theoretical ideas about art.

Harmony in Red, 1908-09

oil on canvas, 70 $^7/_8$ x 78 $^7/_8$ in (180 x 200 cm), The Hermitage, St. Petersburg, Russia

The interior scene and the view through the window have been simplified and flattened by leaving out shadows and details. This makes it look like a tapestry, with a strong decorative pattern made up of color and line.

"A work of art must be harmonious in its entirety."

Henri Matisse, "A Painter's Notes," 1908

Financial Security

THE RUSSIAN BALLET

Shchukin was not Matisse's only Russian patron. Another was Sergei Diaghilev, founder and manager of the Ballets Russes, or Russian Ballet.

Diaghilev's ballet company first came to Paris in 1909. It was a sensational success, admired for its music and dancers as well as its spectacular stage designs by the Russian artists Léon Bakst and Alexandre Benois.

When Diaghilev invited Matisse to design costumes and sets for his production of Igor Stravinsky's *Song of the Nightingale*, the artist welcomed the chance to use costumes as "moving colors." The production eventually had its premier in London in 1920.

The Russian Sergei Shchukin gave Matisse his first major commission. In 1909, he asked the artist to paint an especially large canvas. He was so pleased with the preliminary oil study that Matisse prepared for *Dance* that he commissioned a second picture called *Music*.

A HOUSE AND GARDEN

By now, art had made the forty-year-old Matisse wealthy enough to buy a home at Issy-les-Moulineaux outside of Paris. He and his family moved there in 1909. Matisse had a studio built in the garden, where he painted Shchukin's huge canvases, both almost 14 feet (4 m) long.

▲ Matisse's large house at Issy-les-Moulineaux, set on a 1 acre (4,600 sq m) plot, was an outward sign of his success. He loved the garden, and found inspiration in the colors of the flowers. Here Matisse was able to distance himself from the bustle of Paris, and create a perfect environment in which to paint.

A GALLERY CONTRACT

Wanting to make sure that his income did not depend on purchases by individual collectors, Matisse also signed a contract with one of Paris's leading galleries, Bernheim-Jeune. The gallery agreed to buy all his work at a set rate. His money worries were over.

TIMELINE ▶

1909	1909	1910
Shchukin commissions *Dance* and *Music*. Matisse buys a house at Issy-les-Moulineaux, outside Paris.	Ballets Russes perform in Paris for the first time.	Matisse exhibits at the Bernheim-Jeune Gallery, visits Munich to see important exhibition of Islamic art, and travels to Andalusia in southern Spain.

Dance, 1910

oil on canvas, 102 x 154 in (260 x 391 cm), The Hermitage, St. Petersburg, Russia

Set against a plain background of "the bluest of blues" for the sky, and "the greenest of greens" for the hill, Matisse's huge figures move in a rhythmic circle. Form and color are kept simple, and the graceful lines add to the impression of movement.

*"Three colors for a vast panel of dancers;
blue for the sky, pink for the bodies, green for the hill."*

Henri Matisse

Islamic Influences

From 1910 onward, using the money he had made from the sale of his paintings, Matisse began to travel a lot more. In that year he visited Munich in Germany, to attend a huge exhibition of Islamic art. Matisse was overwhelmed by the beautiful colors and patterns of the textiles, carpets, and ceramics he saw there.

▲ Matisse occasionally had fun putting his own pictures and sculptures into new pictures. Here, in *Goldfish and Sculpture*, 1911, he brings together one of his sculptures of a reclining nude (see page 16) with one of his favorite props, a goldfish bowl.

TRAVELS IN NORTH AFRICA

Probably the most important journeys Matisse made at this time were two long working trips to Morocco in 1911 and 1912. The peaceful painting of a young Moroccan girl on a rooftop in Tangier (see right) reflects Matisse's love of the exotic clothing and bright colors that he found there.

Matisse liked how Islamic art emphasized surface patterns, rather than creating a realistic sense of space and depth, and he does the same in this work. It is a bold composition, in which the kneeling figure, slippers, and goldfish bowl seem to float against the angular pattern of different shades of blue.

STUDIO PROPS

Like many artists, Matisse had favorite objects which he painted. In his studio, he kept various fabrics, carpets, tiles, and ornaments that he had collected in Spain and North Africa. These appear in numerous compositions.

Around the time that he painted *Zorah on the Terrace* (right), Matisse often painted goldfish in his pictures. The goldfish bowl seems out of place on a blazing hot North African roof terrace. Matisse may have included it simply because he felt that its decorative shape and bright color were what the composition needed.

TIMELINE ▶

1911	1912	1913
Matisse visits North Africa. Autumn: he accompanies Shchukin to Moscow. Closes down his art school (see page 16).	Matisse makes another painting trip to Morocco in North Africa.	Matisse exhibits his Moroccan paintings at the Bernheim-Jeune Gallery. Also exhibits at the Armory Show in New York, a huge, controversial exhibition which is said to mark the start of American interest in modern art.

Zorah on the Terrace, 1912
oil on canvas, 45 ⁵/₈ x 39 ³/₈ in (116 x 100 cm), Pushkin
Museum, Moscow, Russia

**Matisse arranged the slippers, goldfish bowl, and central
figure in the picture to form a triangle. This gives the
composition a strong sense of balance. Note how splashes
of red and orange are also carefully balanced.**

*"The revelation came to me
from the Orient."*

Henri Matisse

Inspired by North Africa

When Matisse arrived in Tangier on the North African coast in January of 1912, he was following in the footsteps of many European artists. Like them, Matisse had been attracted by the promise of spectacular scenery and architecture, exotically dressed people, and dazzling natural light. In 1912, Morocco was about to become a French colony but the political situation did not concern Matisse.

▲ This painting, showing the interior of a family home, comes from Eugène Delacroix's *Album of a Voyage to Spain, Morocco, and Algeria*, published in 1834. Delacroix was one of the first European artists to record the exotic scenes of North Africa. His paintings encouraged other artists to follow his example.

NORTH AFRICA

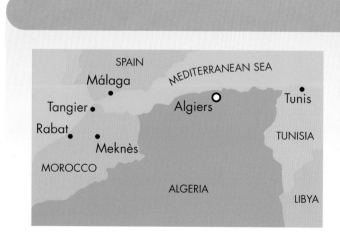

European artists traveling in North Africa can be seen as part of the political and economic colonization of the African continent. While in the late 19th century European powers fought to set up colonies, and traders plundered African diamonds, ivory, and human slaves, artists wanted to seek out the brilliant colors and light. North Africa was relatively easy to get to, being just a short sea crossing from Spain. Until air travel, equally exotic locations that were further away were difficult for all but the most courageous explorers to reach.

EUGENE DELACROIX

The person responsible for making so many Europeans want to travel to North Africa was the Romantic artist, Eugène Delacroix (1798-1863). Eighty years before Matisse, in the early 1830s, Delacroix visited Morocco on a six-month trip that was to inspire his art for the rest of his life. Delacroix had been invited by a French diplomat to make sketches to record his visit to the Sultan. Eventually he completed about eighty pictures.

◀ This Moroccan curved arch, open doorway, and tiled floor are typical of the everyday scenes which inspired Matisse and other artists. Macke used a doorway in his picture below as part of the colorful pattern.

▲ *Turkish Café I*, August Macke, 1914.

A MAGNET FOR ARTISTS

By the time of Matisse's 1912 visit, North Africa had become a magnet for artists. This was partly because of the great Islamic exhibition held in Munich, Germany, in 1910, which opened the eyes of many people to the beauty and variety of Islamic art.

IN MATISSE'S FOOTSTEPS

Two years after Matisse's 1912 visit, a group of artist friends, Paul Klee (1879-1940), Louis Moillet (1880-1962), and August Macke (1887-1914), spent just two weeks in Tunisia in North Africa.

That was enough, however, to transform Klee from an artist who worked mainly in black and white into someone who was famous for his extraordinary use of color. "Color and I are at one," he said.

The trip to Tunisia also inspired Macke to produce what many consider his finest works, one of which is shown on the left. Sadly, in that same year, Macke was killed in action in World War I. He was just twenty-seven years old.

A Darker World

NORTH POLE AND SOUTH POLE

Western art in the first half of the 20th century was dominated by two names, Henri Matisse and Pablo Picasso (1881-1973). While Matisse changed the way color was used, Picasso revolutionized the way artists showed form.

Having come to Paris from his native country Spain in 1904, Picasso soon joined the circle of avant-garde artists who were exploring new ideas in painting and sculpture. He and Matisse met at Gertrude Stein's apartment in 1906. Despite being complete opposites – "as different as the North Pole is from the South Pole," to quote Matisse – the two men became and remained both friends and rivals.

▲ This photograph of Picasso was taken at his Paris studio in 1916.

Matisse's travels were brought to an abrupt end with the outbreak of World War I in 1914. Although he avoided creating images of war, the war had a powerful impact on his paintings. Matisse began using darker colors and harsher, geometric compositions which seem to express his sadness.

▲ When war broke out Matisse's son Pierre volunteered for the tank corps. Tanks, such as this French Renault FT17 photographed in a German street, were still a recent invention. Matisse also volunteered for military service, but was turned down because at forty-four he was considered too old.

The large, stark painting (right), showing his younger son Pierre at the piano, is a far cry from the "comforting" art Matisse had dreamed of creating (see page 18). As well as expressing a new feeling of unease, the painting shows how Matisse responded to the Cubist art of Picasso and Braque, particularly in the way that one side of Pierre's face has been reduced to blank triangles.

TIMELINE ▶

1914	1915	1916	1917	1918
August 3rd: World War I breaks out. Matisse's work on exhibition in Berlin is seized. Matisse is turned down for military service. Late August: Paris under threat from German army. Matisse and family travel south to Toulouse and Collioure.	Matisse paints fewer pictures but makes many etchings.	Matisse exhibits in London. He spends his first winter on the Riviera in Nice.	During the winter, Matisse visits the elderly Impressionist artist Auguste Renoir in Cagnes. Russian Revolution brings down the Russian Empire.	World War I ends.

The Piano Lesson, 1916

oil on canvas, 96 ¹/₂ x 83 ³/₄ in (245.1 x 212.7 cm), Museum of Modern Art, New York, New York

Matisse uses angular shapes to create an uncomfortable, disjointed composition, but softens the effect with the gentle curls of the window grille and music stand.

Winters on the Riviera

◀ A modern photograph of a dancer in North Africa. She is wearing the sort of brightly colored, flowing costume that many European painters tried to capture on canvas.

From 1914 onward, Matisse often visited southern France. While remaining at his home in Issy for the rest of the year, he soon began to spend the winter months each year on the Riviera in Nice, where it was warmer. In Nice, Matisse found peace, and the "soft and delicate light" which inspired him throughout his life. Initially he stayed in sea front hotels, and would begin each day with an hour's violin practice (he was an excellent violinist) before painting in his room or outdoors until the evening.

◀ This photograph of Matisse working in his apartment was taken in Nice in 1928. Matisse has posed his model, dressed as an odalisque, in front of brightly patterned curtains. A similar arrangement was used for the painting opposite.

WOMEN OF THE HAREM

"Odalisques" were the women who lived in a sultan or rich man's "harem," or private quarters, hidden away from the outside world. Guarded by slaves inside the house, groups of odalisques spent their days bathing or lounging together. Their mysterious lives and exotic clothes made them very appealing to European and American imaginations.

"As for odalisques, I had seen them in Morocco, and so was able to put them in my pictures back in France," wrote Matisse. In fact, although Matisse might have seen similar-looking women, he would not have been allowed to see an odalisque. They were in the "harem," and kept hidden from the view of outsiders.

In 1921, Matisse rented an apartment in Nice where he created a decorative world of patterned wallpaper, wall hangings, and exotic fabrics and carpets, in which he posed his models. Here, he painted many fantasy pictures of "odalisques," or harem women, including the stunningly decorated picture opposite.

TIMELINE ▶

1920	1921	1925
The Ballets Russes' production of *Song of the Nightingale* is premiered in London, with costumes and sets designed by Matisse. Matisse visits London, and Etretat on the Normandy coast.	Matisse rents an apartment in Place Charles-Félix in Nice, where he paints his odalisque pictures. Also spends time in Paris and Etretat.	Matisse visits Italy with his wife, his daughter, and her husband.

Decorative Figure on an Ornamental Ground, 1925

oil on canvas, 51 1/8 x 38 5/8 in (131 x 98 cm), Musée National d'Art Moderne, Pompidou Center, Paris, France

Notice how many different patterns Matisse has used for the "ornamental background." Swirling curves and floral designs contrast well with the angular lines of the figure.

Crossing the Atlantic

In March of 1930, Matisse went to Tahiti. He stopped in the U.S. along the way and wrote that he was tempted to "go no further than New York, so impressed am I with this new world. It's big and majestic, like the sea." He found Tahiti to be very hot and humid. Matisse said that he "did absolutely nothing, except take bad photographs."

Matisse returned to France in July, but crossed the Atlantic again a few months later to serve on a jury for the prestigious Carnegie prize. Afterward, he went to Merion, Pennsylvania, to see Dr. Albert Barnes. Barnes had commissioned Matisse to paint a mural – *The Dance* – for his art foundation.

▲ Pictures on display from the Barnes collection. After Dr. Barnes's death in 1951, the public was not allowed to see his collection. In 1993-94, following court action, some of the collection went on tour for the first time, to France and Japan.

A NEW TECHNIQUE

Matisse had never worked on such a big painting before. In order to make planning the painting easier, he began using cutout pieces of colored paper, which he could arrange and rearrange. Although, originally a labor-saving technique, Matisse's use of the paper cutout was to become an art form in its own right.

THE BARNES FOUNDATION

Multi-millionaire Albert Barnes made his fortune by inventing the antiseptic "Argyrol." He used his money to collect art and bought Leo Stein's collection. When the stock market collapsed in 1929, it brought financial ruin to many, and triggered the Great Depression. This allowed Barnes to buy major works of art very cheaply. He eventually owned, among many other works, about 120 Cézannes, 200 Renoirs, 95 Picassos, and more than 100 Matisses.

In 1922, he established the Barnes Foundation at the mansion he had built to house his collection. His aim was to provide students from all ethnic backgrounds with an education in art appreciation.

For years Barnes's spectacular collection remained a hidden treasure trove. It was only in the 1990s that some of the works were loaned and reproduced for the first time.

TIMELINE ▶

1927	1929	1930	1931	1933
Matisse is awarded the U.S. Carnegie prize. He exhibits in New York.	Wall Street Crash (U.S. stock market collapses).	Matisse travels to Tahiti via the U.S., back to France, then to the U.S. again to serve on jury for the Carnegie prize (Picasso wins). Barnes commissions *The Dance* mural.	Matisse uses paper cutouts on Barnes mural to make revisions easier.	Barnes mural is finally completed in May. Matisse takes the summer off.

"Expression and decoration are one and the same thing."

Henri Matisse

Study for The Dance, 1932-33

Gouache on cut and pasted paper, 13 x 34 in (33 x 88 cm), The Barnes Foundation, Merion, Pennsylvania, First version of *The Dance* (*Dance I*)

The Dance was designed to fit into three arch shapes above windows in the Barnes Foundation building at Merion, Pennsylvania. It was so huge that Matisse rented a one-time film studio (top) in Nice to work on it. Having completed the work (called *Dance I*), he discovered that he had been given the wrong measurements and had to make a second version.

Making It Simpler

Matisse was now in his sixties. He found that the three years he had spent working on *The Dance* had taken their toll on his health. In 1933, having seen the painting put into place, he took the summer off to recover. Around this time, he became interested in creating book illustrations, tapestry designs, etchings, and drawings.

THE CONE SISTERS

The Pink Nude is part of a collection made by two American sisters from Baltimore, Claribel (1864-1929) and Etta Cone (1870-1949). Etta's formal education ended when she left high school, but Claribel was one of the then rare women who went on to further education. She studied medicine, and later worked in Germany.

On a visit to Paris, Etta was introduced to the Steins (see page 12), and through them, to Matisse and Picasso.

After World War I (1914-18), during which the family textile business flourished, Claribel returned from Germany and the Cone sisters began to travel abroad and gather a magnificent collection of modern art.

◄ A photograph taken by Matisse showing Lydia sitting in front of *The Pink Nude*, October 1935.

Between May and October of that year, Matisse photographed more than twenty stages of this painting. The image started out looking much more realistic, but Matisse gradually simplified and emphasized the shapes until they became almost an abstract pattern.

▲ Dr. Claribel Cone, the elder of the two Cone sisters.

In the early 1930s, Matisse hired a young Russian woman, Lydia Delectorskaya, as an assistant. She became his companion, secretary, and model, and was to stay with him until his death. Lydia modeled for many paintings, including *The Pink Nude* (right). She and Matisse took photographs of the successive stages of this and other works. They show how much effort Matisse put into the process of simplifying the elements of a picture until, as he wrote, "I see nothing more in it than I want."

TIMELINE ▶

1934	1935	1937	1938
Matisse begins work on illustrations for the U.S. edition of James Joyce's *Ulysses*.	Lydia Delectorskaya is hired as an assistant. She models for *The Pink Nude* and other works. Matisse sends Etta Cone photographs of *The Pink Nude*'s progress.	Matisse is ill and goes into the hospital. His marriage to Amélie ends. He designs scenery and costumes for Ballets Russes' production of *Red and Black*.	Matisse moves to Hôtel Régina in Cimiez, near Nice.

The Pink Nude, 1935

oil on canvas, 26 x 36¹/₂ in (66 x 92 cm), Baltimore Museum of Art, Cone Collection, Baltimore, Maryland

Outlined in black, the pink nude fills almost the entire canvas, and looks monumental despite the relatively small size of the painting. The background details have been reduced to an overall grid-like pattern, and the flowers that can be seen in the earlier versions have become simplified into abstract shapes.

"I don't paint women. I paint pictures."

Henri Matisse

Harmony Shattered

▲ During the Nazi occupation of France, the French Resistance carried out many acts of sabotage, such as derailing this train.

THE FRENCH RESISTANCE

Matisse was an ailing, elderly man when the German Nazis invaded and occupied France. He seems to have tried to ignore the horrors that were happening in his country. However, his wife and daughter responded differently. They joined the French Resistance, which was the secret movement dedicated to fighting the Nazis.

Members of the Resistance knew they were risking their lives. In May of 1944, Matisse wrote to a friend, "I have just received the biggest shock of my life... My wife and daughter have been arrrested." Amélie was sentenced to six months in prison. His daughter, Marguerite, was tortured but escaped. She spent several weeks in hiding before returning to Paris, which had been liberated by Allied troops in August of 1944. Early in 1945, she visited her father in the south. He made several drawings of her and donated two of them to the Resistance movement.

Combining two of Matisse's favorite themes – women and music – the painting opposite gives the feeling of harmonious calm. This is surprising since it was painted in the year that Europe was thrown into turmoil with the outbreak of World War II. Also, at seventy years old, Matisse was ill and living apart from his wife.

UNCERTAINTY

When German troops invaded France in 1940, Matisse canceled a trip to Brazil. As he wrote, he would have felt "like a deserter" if he left the country. In 1941, he was operated on for stomach cancer. Two years later, when Nice had become a potential bombing target for the Allies fighting Germany, he moved out to the nearby town of Vence, to a villa called "Le Rêve," or "The Dream."

◄ In November of 1938, Matisse moved into a room at the Hôtel Régina, situated in the hills above Nice, at Cimiez. He moved out to Vence during World War II, but returned to live and work here from 1949 until his death in 1954.

TIMELINE ▶

1939	1941	1943	1944	1945
Matisse visits Geneva. World War II starts.	Both U.S. and USSR enter the war. Matisse undergoes surgery for cancer.	Matisse moves to "Le Rêve," a villa in Vence.	Matisse begins paper cutout illustrations for *Jazz*. His wife and daughter are arrested. Paris is liberated by Allied troops.	World War II ends. Matisse retrospective exhibition in Paris. Combined Matisse-Picasso exhibition in London.

Music, 1939

oil on canvas, 45 3/8 x 45 3/8 in (115 x 115.1 cm), Albright-Knox Art Gallery, Buffalo, New York

Matisse gradually simplified the figures, creating sweeping curves that echo each other and link the figures and the background behind them. Notice how he has distorted the foot of the figure on the right below the zig-zagged hem of her fashionable pants.

"My drawings and my canvases are parts of myself."

Henri Matisse

The French Riviera

The French Riviera extends from St. Tropez in the west to the Italian border in the east. This beautiful stretch of coastline is sometimes known as the Côte d' Azur, or Azur Coast. It is backed by dramatic mountains, lapped by the warm Mediterranean Sea, and bathed in almost year-round sunshine. Unsurprisingly, it is one of the most glamorous vacation resorts in the world, and home to the rich and famous including artists, film stars, and the jet set.

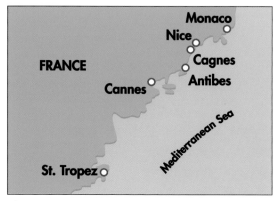

▲ This map shows Nice, Cannes, and the major towns along the French Riviera.

▲ The Riviera was a winter haven before it became a summer resort.

WINTER SUNSHINE

When Matisse first stayed on the Riviera in 1916, it had already been transformed into a winter home for the members of high society. Throughout the 19th century, wealthy visitors from Britain had come here, making the long journey by steamship or horse and carriage. Trains eventually reached Cannes in 1863, which made the trip much more comfortable.

A HEALTH RESORT

The most famous Victorian visitor was Queen Victoria. She regularly took the train to the Riviera with her son, Prince Leopold, in an attempt to cure his tuberculosis. The mild climate attracted invalids as well as vacationers. The artist Renoir (1841-1919), who moved to Cagnes partly to find relief from the rheumatism that was crippling him, called the Riviera "a hot house in which fragile people take refuge."

▲ A 1963 photograph of Cannes during film festival fortnight. The festival has attracted Hollywood glamour to the Riviera.

THE POPULARITY OF NICE

In Victorian times, the town of Nice was a popular resort area, and many stately hotels were built there, including Matisse's home, the Hôtel Régina. Although the British started the trend, the Riviera soon became a magnet for other members of European royalty and aristocracy. Artists and writers also were attracted by the lifestyle and the sunlight there.

A GLAMOROUS PLAYGROUND

After World War I, Americans arrived and transformed the Riviera into a year-round playground for the fabulously rich.

In the 1920s swimming and sunbathing became fashionable. People started to associate a golden tan with health.

THE CANNES FILM FESTIVAL

The outbreak of World War II in 1939 brought the partying to an end. However, in 1946, the year after the war ended, the first Cannes Film Festival began a link between the Riviera and the movie industry which still remains strong today.

While film stars and rock stars continue to enjoy the pleasures of the Riviera, it has also become a popular resort for everyday vacationers.

A Final Flowering

After his cancer operations, Matisse became friends with the young nurse who cared for him. She later became a nun, Sister Jacques-Marie. She asked Matisse to help with designs for a chapel they were building near where he was staying in Vence.

Matisse took on the project with enthusiasm. He made designs from paper cutouts for the stained glass windows, while the plain wall tiles were decorated with simple line drawings.

Even though Matisse did not have strong religious beliefs, he felt that working in the chapel was the culmination of his life's work, which expressed what he called "the nearly religious feeling I have for life."

▲ Crippled by illness, Matisse creates a shape cutout of colored paper. "Color" and what he called "the curve" were the basic elements of his art.

▲ Matisse (right) in the Chapel at Vence, May 1951.

Just as Matisse's painting ability first blossomed in 1890 while he was recovering from appendicitis, so the final flowering of his art was partly a result of a similar, though much more serious operation, for cancer. After the operation, Matisse could no longer stand at an easel. However, sitting in bed or in his wheelchair, he could cut out paper that had been colored with gouache, or opaque watercolor. He was then able to position the pieces as he wanted, or direct his assistants to position them.

Some of Matisse's most original and wonderful works, such as *The Snail* (opposite), were created in this way during his final years. "Paper cutouts allow me to draw directly in color," he wrote, "...one movement linking line with color." Matisse carried on with this unique art form right up until the end. He was using paper cutouts to work on the designs for a stained glass window for a chapel in New York when he died on November 3, 1954.

TIMELINE ▶

1947	1947	1949	1951	1952	1954
Made Commander of the Legion of Honor. Deaths of Bonnard and Marquet.	Matisse devotes himself to decorating the Chapel of the Rosary in Vence.	Matisse moves back into the Hôtel Régina.	Chapel at Vence completed. Exhibitions in New York, Chicago, San Francisco, Tokyo.	Matisse Museum opens at Le Cateau-Cambrésis. Matisse creates a series of cutouts, *Blue Nudes*.	November 3rd Matisse dies. He is buried in Cimiez cemetery.

The Snail, 1953

Gouache on cut and pasted paper, 112 ³/₄ x 113 in (287 x 288 cm), Tate Modern, London, England

Although this huge picture may look like an abstract spiral pattern, Matisse explained how it was based on an actual snail. "First of all I drew the snail from nature, holding it in my hand. I became aware of an unfolding. I found an image in my mind purified of the shell."

Matisse's Legacy

Matisse was one of the most important artists of the 20th century. His continuing influence can be seen throughout the art world. The roots of Expressionism and Abstract Art, two major movements in 20th-century art, can both be found in his work.

COLOR AND FORM

Matisse was particularly influential in the way he used color and in his attitude toward form, or shape.

Matisse rejected the idea that artists should reproduce what they see with realistic colors. "The chief aim of color," he wrote, "should be to serve expression. To paint an autumn landscape I will not try to remember what colors suit that season; I will be inspired only by the feeling it arouses in me."

Later in his life, Matisse also began to simplify form more, often making the original subject unrecognizable – as he did with *The Snail* (see previous page).

FOLLOWING MATISSE

Many abstract painters have been influenced by Matisse's use of color, form, and pattern. Among them is Kenneth Noland (b. 1924), a leading figure in an American art movement called Color Field Painting – a form of Abstract Expressionism which uses pure, unmodeled areas of color. In the 1960s he developed a style called Hard Edge painting (see above).

In 2001, Noland acknowledged the influence that Matisse had on his own work. "He's the one I've learnt the most from ... I hesitate to say this, but there's an argument that Matisse might have been the greatest artist in Western art."

▲ This example of Kenneth Noland's Hard Edge painting was created after 1962. The geometric form and bold stripes of pure color in this pattern create an exciting and dramatic picture. The effect is enhanced by the unusual diamond-shaped canvas on which it is painted.

Matisse's paper cutouts were also influential. Never before had collage been used on such a grand scale and achieved such beauty. Romare Bearden (1912-88), the African American Civil Rights activist and artist, greatly admired Matisse. In the 1960s he made large-scale collages which combined cut-up photographic images with areas of flat color made from cut-up colored paper. One of them is reproduced on the right.

MATISSE MUSEUM, NICE

Created in 1963, the Matisse Museum is housed on the upper floors of a 17th-century villa (see below) situated in the hills above Nice. In 1993, a project was underway to renovate and develop the site. A new extension was built which greatly increased the gallery space. The museum has 68 cutout paintings, 236 drawings, 218 engravings, and 57 sculptures on permanent display – making it one of the largest collections of Matisse's work in the world.

▲ *Poseidon The Sea God – Enemy of Odysseus*, 1977, a collage by the American artist Romare Bearden.

◀ The Matisse Museum in Nice. The museum is housed in a 17th-century villa which was not designed to display works of art. However, the villa has very high ceilings and on summer days the rooms are flooded with the clear Mediterranean light that once captured Matisse's imagination.

Letters to a Friend

In general, artists do not work in isolation. They enjoy sharing ideas with each other and discussing the theories that fuel their passion for art – perhaps over coffee or in an exchange of letters.

During his lifetime Matisse wrote many letters. An interesting record exists of his correspondence with the artist Pierre Bonnard (1867-1947). Excerpts from these letters bring to life their close friendship and help to illustrate events that were important to them at the time.

> *Dear friend,*
> *I'm taking the boat for Panama in a week. Will be in Nice around the end of July. Been a good stay and a good rest. Saw all sorts of things. Will tell you about it. Lived twenty days on a coral isle: pure light, pure color: diamond, sapphire, emerald, turquoise. Prodigious fish. Accomplished absolutely nothing except bad photos. Good health to both. Will be glad to see France again.*
> *Henri Matisse*

▲ Pierre Bonnard at work in his studio.

◀ Tahiti Papeete, June 6, 1930. This letter conveys some of the excitement felt by Matisse when he saw the exotic colors of the South Pacific.

PIERRE BONNARD

Bonnard was two years older than Matisse, and like him had studied law before attending the Académie Julian and the Ecole des Beaux-Arts. As with Matisse, color was important to Bonnard, although his style creates a very different effect. Bonnard's work focuses on quiet, intimate, domestic scenes, often showing his beloved wife Martha bathing. In many of Bonnard's paintings there is a shimmering light which seems to dissolve form and emphasize flat, decorative pattern. Despite their different styles, both men believed that the role of painting was not to copy nature, but to express the artist's response to what he saw.

TIMELINE ▶

1869	1900	1905	1908	1911	1914
December 31, 1869 Matisse is born at Le Cateau-Cambrésis.	**1900** Works as a decorator for the Universal Exhibition.	**1905** Paints with Derain at Collioure. Exhibits with group, the "Fauves."	**1908** Travels to Germany, exhibits in New York, Moscow. Sells to Shchukin. Publishes "A Painter's Notes."	**1911** Visits North Africa, accompanies Shchukin to Moscow. Closes art school.	**1914** Works in Berlin are seized. Turned down for military service. Travels with family to Toulouse, Collioure.
1887 Moves to Paris to study law.	**1901** Exhibits at Salon des Indépendants.	**1906** Sells painting to Leo Stein. Meets Picasso.	**1909** Commission from Shchukin. Ballets Russes come to Paris.	**1912** Trip to Morocco.	**1915** Only does a few paintings, but lots of etchings.
1890 Is ill with appendicitis. While recovering starts painting.	**1903** The first Salon d'Automne.	**1907** Exchanges paintings with Picasso. Visits Italy.	**1910** Exhibits at Bernheim-Jeune. Visits Germany. Travels to Andalusia, Spain.	**1913** Moroccan paintings at Bernheim-Jeune. Exhibits in New York at controversial Armory Show.	**1916** Exhibits in London. Winter in Nice.
1891 Returns to Paris to study art. Joins the Académie Julian.	**1904** Exhibits at Vollard's Gallery. Summer in the south of France where influenced by Signac.	**1908** Opens art school in Paris.		**1914** World War I begins.	**1917** Visits Renoir.

During World War II, Matisse and Bonnard were near-neighbors in southern France. Their letters show how much they enjoyed each other's company, and also the pleasure they had seeing each other's paintings.

My dear Matisse,
It is quite cold in Cannes, the kind of cold that jars and weakens...I hope that soon the sun will warm us a little again, and I fully intend to come and see you in Nice. I really need to see another kind of painting besides my own. My friendliest wishes, Bonnard

▲ **February 9, 1940. Proof that it wasn't always warm on the French Riviera.**

My dear Bonnard,
I have been back in Nice for some ten days ... there is a general anguish about Nice soon being occupied [by the Nazis] and it affects me so much my work is difficult. I believe a visit to you would do me the greatest good. Certainly the sight of your paintings would lighten the wall in front of my nose ... But how can I get up to Le Cannet? Bus or train to Cannes, and then what? Is there a taxi or horsecar or bus that goes to your house?

My dear Matisse,
Your two pictures decorate (that's the word) my dining room, against an ochre background that suits them. Especially the woman with the necklace – the red is wonderful late in the afternoon. By day it is the blue that takes the lead. What an intense life the colors have, and how they vary with the light! I make discoveries every day, and I thank you for this pleasure and this instruction. Yours, Bonnard

◀ **September 7, 1940. Matisse describes his fear of the Nazi advance and also the difficulties of travel in wartime.**

▲ **This letter written in 1946 expresses Bonnard's high regard for Matisse's art.**

1918	1927	1933	1939	1945	1951
November 11, 1918 World War I ends.	**1927** Awarded Carnegie prize. Exhibits in New York.	**1933** Barnes mural completed. Summer off.	**1939** Visits Geneva. World War II begins.	**1945** World War II ends. Matisse retrospective exhibition in Paris. Joint exhibition with Picasso in London.	**1951** Vence chapel complete. Exhibitions in New York, San Francisco, Chicago, and Tokyo.
1920 *Song of the Nightingale* premier, with sets by Matisse. Visits London, Etretat in Normandy.	**1929** Wall Street Crash.	**1934** Illustrations for Joyce's *Ulysses*.	**1941** U.S., USSR enter the war. Has surgery for cancer.		
	1930 Travels to Tahiti, twice to U.S. On jury for Carnegie prize. Commissioned by Barnes to do mural.	**1935** Hires Lydia Delectorskaya.	**1943** Moves to Vence.	**1947** Commander of the Legion of Honor. Works on chapel in Vence.	**1952** Matisse Museum opens at Le Cateau-Cambrésis. Does series of paper cutouts, *Blue Nudes*.
1921 Rents apartment in Nice. Spends time in Paris and Etretat.		**1937** In hospital. His marriage ends. Designs for Ballets Russes.	**1944** Works with paper cutouts. Wife and daughter arrested by Nazis. Paris liberated by Allies.		
1925 Family visit to Italy.	**1931** First use of paper cutouts, for planning mural.	**1938** Moves to Hôtel Régina, Cimiez (Nice).		**1949** Moves back into Hôtel Régina at Cimiez.	**November 3, 1954** Matisse dies. Buried in Cimiez cemetery.

Glossary

abstract: art that does not imitate the world around us. It is usually impossible to recognize objects, people, or places in abstract art.

Ballets Russes: a ballet company created by Sergei Diaghilev (1872-1929). It worked closely with many of the most important contemporary artists and composers, including Matisse and the composer Igor Stravinsky.

Carnegie prize: the prize awarded to a living artist by the Carnegie Foundation, in honor of the philanthropist Andrew Carnegie (1839-1919).

ceramics: artwork created by baking clay.

collage: a technique in which pieces of paper, fabric, etc. are glued onto a surface to create a picture. (From the French word *colle*, meaning paste or glue.)

commission: to place an order for a work of art.

Cubism: the name of an art movement based in Paris from about 1907 onward led by Pablo Picasso (1881-1973) and Georges Braque (1882-1963). The Cubists painted multiple viewpoints of a person or object so that they all could be seen at the same time.

Ecole des Beaux-Arts: a prominent art school in Paris.

etching: a print on paper made from an engraved metal plate.

exotic: foreign, different or unusual.

Expressionism: an approach to painting that communicates an emotional state of mind rather than external reality. The Norwegian artist Edvard Munch (1863-1944), who painted *The Scream*, was a leading Expressionist.

Fauves: the name given by a scandalized critic in 1905 to a group of painters including Matisse, André Derain, and Maurice de Vlaminck.

foundation: an organization that distributes private wealth for the benefit of the public. Foundations active in the arts include Carnegie and Rockefeller.

Impressionists: a group of artists based in Paris during the late 19th century who painted "impressions" of the world with broad brushstrokes of pure color. The group included Auguste Renoir (1841-1919), Claude Monet (1840-1926), and Edgar Degas (1834-1917).

Islamic: associated with the religion of Islam. Islamic art is ornamental and abstract in style.

Legion of Honor: French award given for outstanding civil or military service.

naturalistic: describes art that attempts to copy nature as closely as possible.

Nazi: short for National Socialist, the extreme right-wing political party led by Adolf Hitler that ruled Germany from 1933 to 1945.

Neo-Impressionism: a painting style related to Impressionism. Its goal was to increase the sense of light and color by applying unmixed colors in small dots.

Old Masters: the name given to the great European painters from the period 1500-1800, including Leonardo da Vinci (1452-1519), Raphael (1483-1520), Michelangelo (1475-1564), and Caravaggio (1571-1610).

patron: someone who supports an artist financially by buying their work or giving them money.

Post-Impressionists: a group of mostly French artists, although it includes Dutchman Vincent van Gogh (1853-90), who were inspired and influenced by the Impressionists' use of pure color.

Romantic: describes a movement affecting art, literature, and music between c. 1780 and 1840, which went against the strict traditions of classicism and toward a more picturesque and imaginative style.

Salon: annual art exhibition organized by the French Academy. In the 19th century the jury refused works by many Impressionist and Post-Impressionist painters, who then exhibited at the Salon des Refusés. The Salon des Indépendants was started in 1884.

Surrealism: an art movement that emerged in the 1920s that tried to depict the life of our subconscious minds, or dreams. Its most famous artist is Salvador Dali (1904-89).

Museums and Galleries

Works by Matisse are exhibited in museums and galleries all around the world. Some of the ones listed here are devoted solely to Matisse, but most have a wide range of other artists' works on display.

Even if you can't visit any of these galleries yourself, you may be able to visit their web sites. Gallery web sites often show pictures of the artworks they have on display. Some of the web sites even offer virtual tours which allow you to wander around and look at different paintings while sitting comfortably in front of your computer! Most of the international web sites listed below include an option that allows you to view them in English.

Albright-Knox Art Gallery
1285 Elmwood Avenue
Buffalo, NY 14222-1096
www.albrightknox.org

The Baltimore Museum of Art
10 Art Museum Drive
Baltimore, MD 21218-3898
www.artbma.org

The Barnes Foundation
300 North Latch's Lane
Merion, PA 19066
www.barnesfoundation.org

Center National d'Art et de Culture Georges Pompidou
75191 Paris
cedex 04
France
www.centrepompidou.fr/english

Musée Matisse
164 avenue des Arènes de Cimiez
Nice
France
www.musee-matisse-nice.org

Musée Matisse
Palais Fénelon
59360 Le Cateau-Cambrésis
France
e-mail: museematisse@cg59.fr

Musée d'Orsay
62 rue de Lille
75343 Paris
cedex 07 France
www.musee-orsay.fr

The Museum of Modern Art
(Under renovation until 2005.
See web site for further details.)
11 West 53 Street
New York, NY
www.moma.org

The National Pushkin Museum
The English version of this site is currently under construction
www.museumpushkin.ru

Statens Museum for Kunst
The Secretariat
Sølvgade 48-50
DK-1307 Copenhagen K
Denmark
www.smk.dk

The State Hermitage Museum
34 Dvortsovaya Embankment
St Petersburg 190000
Russia
www.hermitagemuseum.org

Tate Modern
Bankside
London
SE1 9TG
www.tate.org.uk/modern/default.htm

Index